366 Affirmations and Inspirations to Live By

Phyllis Okon

Paperback. ISBN: 978-1-950080-13-7

For my family- You are my magick

Foreword

I ain't tellin' no lie
Mine's a tale that can't be told
My freedom I hold dear
How years ago in days of old
When magic filled the air.
— Led Zeppelin

Led Zeppelin is one of the greatest rock bands of all time. Their lyrics have been listened to for generations. My kids are listening to Led Zeppelin right now. This particular song, Ramble On, always had me thinking. Robert Plant sings about When magic filled the air, as in magic was something that happened long ago, in days of old.

I hate to break it to you, Robert, but nothing has changed. Magic is all around us, even today. Each one of us has the capability of transforming our lives to live a life we truly desire. Magic was never a thing of the past. It was always around. We just lost touch with it.

The problem is that we've changed. Humanity. Society. Everything has shifted from fulfilling your dreams to turning the invisible into the visible. I'm not blaming anyone. It's no one's fault in particular. The world has gotten crazier and more obscure as the years have passed. Our surroundings have changed. They've turned weirder. Again, there is nothing we could have done to change that. We can't control the weather.

Social media dominates our lives. The pandemic changed everything. We are connecting with people over computers as opposed to socializing in person. Many are working from home. Instead of getting more spiritual, we have done the opposite and moved away from our spiritual practices.

I'm here to bring you back to the center. Humanity has veered off course instead of going right down the center. We lost our place and forgot about spiritual teachings. NOW is the time to become more spiritual than ever. Instead of freaking out about what the news said or what has popped up on your *For You* page, we must find that centeredness. We need to program our minds for what we desire in this life. We must learn to stop being distracted by the minutiae of living daily and get back to affirming what's essential.

Enter Phyllis Okon, my wonderful mother. During the crazy times in 2020, Mom learned how to become a psychic and evidential medium while navigating our family-owned multi-million dollar company through extraordinarily rough waters. She lost weight, regained her health, wrote a dozen books, and traveled to distant lands to feed her soul and build her business. All while never missing a grandchild's birthday, event, or an episode of *90-Day Fiancée.*

Mom knows her stuff. Phyllis doesn't lose her way, even when the world is in its darkest days. She is a shining beacon of light for hundreds of people. Mom always retains her spirituality. She has spoken her world into existence and does it with affirmations.

Affirmations are talking about things that are not here but believing and seeing them as real. I am affirming the things around me. *I have money. I live in good health. I am always safe. My life is filled with abundance…*

Wallace Wattles, the great author of *The Science of Getting Rich*, once said in his book:

"Every person has the natural and inherent power to think what they want to think, but it requires far more effort to do so than it does to think the thoughts which are suggested by appearance. To think according to appearance is easy; to think truth regardless of appearance is laborious and requires the expenditure of more power than any other work a person is called to perform.

There is no labor from which most people shrink as they do from that of sustained and consecutive thought; it is the hardest work in the world. This is especially true when truth is contrary to appearances. Every appearance in the visible world tends to produce a corresponding form in the mind which observes it; and this can only be prevented by holding the thought of truth.

To think rich when in the midst of appearances of poverty requires power, but those who acquire this power become a mastermind. They can conquer fate; they can have what they want."

Negative nellies surround us. They are the people who bring us down—energy vampires. Social media makes you think you're doing everything incorrectly. We are surrounded by news that only tells us about the bad things in the world.

Now is your time to conquer your surroundings. Rise above the noise and center yourself. And I am NOT talking about meditation. While meditation may have its benefits, I want actual results, fast.

You are an alchemist. You have an opportunity to turn metal into gold. Transform that cold, faded, weighted anchor of despair and doubt into a shiny, bright object that attracts whatever they want into your life. The change must come from within.

The answer is affirmations.

Listen to what Phyllis has put down in this book. Learn from someone who has applied affirmations to their daily life to acquire everything they need to live an extraordinary life.

I certainly did.

Michael Okon

September 30th, 2023
Oyster Bay Cove, NY
Author of *Just Ask The Universe: A No-Nonsense Guide to Manifesting Your Dreams*

Success only comes to those who dare to attempt."

— Mallika Tripathi

"Life is 10% what happens to you and 90% how you react to it."

— Charles R. Swindoll

The past is in the past, and my past doesn't predict my future.

My heart is open to helpfulness from myself as well as from others.

Changing my mind is a strength,
and does not show weakness.

I have come farther than I ever thought I could, and I'm learning along the way.

I am enough as I am.

Art and music enhance my life.

I know my value.

"By being yourself, you put something wonderful in the world that was not there before."
— Edwin Elliot

I have all that I need to succeed.

No is my boundary, and I am allowed to say it without explanation.

When I look into the mirror,
I see goodness and peace.

My body is beautiful,
no matter its size or shape.

I use compassion to overcome adversity.

I release what no longer serves me.

Today, I will see the world with new eyes.

"Aim for the moon. If you miss, you may hit a star."
— W. Clement Stone

I have the power to create change.

Each day begins with limitless potential.

Rain feeds the flowers. The universe feeds me.

Sometimes, it costs too much to win.

I am free from anxiety and fear.

I forgive all those who have hurt me.
Their words have no impact on my soul.

I breathe deep peace and
surround myself with beauty.

I am a work in progress and
enjoy watching myself grow.

"Talk to yourself like someone you love."
— Brené Brown

Change is good.

I will squeeze every ounce of value
from each day of my life.

I will finish what matters
and let go of what does not.

I will follow my instincts and have no regrets.

I am not afraid to accept my limits.

Difficult times build my character and strength.

I will manifest what makes me happy.

I do not have to be perfect.

My imperfections make me stronger.

I am the captain of my life. I hold the power.

I am able to live my life in balance.

Doors are opening for me.

If the shoes are uncomfortable, I will change them.

I can do anything.

Today is for dreaming.

"Life isn't about finding yourself. Life is about creating yourself."
— George Bernard Shaw

I am prepared for everything that comes my way.

I will wake up motivated and filled with joy.

Challenges are preparing me for
better things to come.

My potential is limitless.

I surround myself with the white light of protection so negativity won't affect me.

I forgive myself.

I love what I love, and that's okay.

I am more than what others see.

"You can't cross the sea merely by standing and staring at the water."
— Rabindranath Tagore

If I choose to be sad, it's my decision.

I breathe in happiness and breathe out negativity.

I will not engage with those
who don't appreciate me.

Today, I will do what I want.

I am grateful for all I have.

Tomorrow is a goal I have yet to achieve,
but I will enjoy thinking about it.

There are no such things as mistakes,
only corrections.

I let go of my expectations
and will enjoy the journey.

"You don't always need a plan. Sometimes you just need to breathe, trust, let go, and see what happens."
— Mandy Hale

Thoughts are things,

and I can make them happen.

I will embrace all changes in my life.

I will surround myself with people
who bring out the best in me.

I have an attitude of gratitude.

I am strong, balanced, and secure.

I do not rise or fall for another.

I am as proud of my accomplishments as I am of my failures, for I have learned from them.

I am full of grace.

My life is a gift, and I appreciate every minute.

Quiet days are good.

Self-reflection, not self-absorption.

I love all my body parts, and they love me.

My feelings and emotions are valid.

I will not let others control my happiness.

"Be there for others, but never leave yourself behind."
— Dodinsky

I will not be anyone but myself.

My higher self connects to me through intuition.

I am listening and open to the messages from the Universe.

I feel loved, even if I am alone.

I do not have to sit in my anger.

I will not allow my life
to be dictated by obligations.

Today, I will enjoy being spontaneous.

I am responsible only for my happiness.

"You don't always need to understand the journey in your life, and you need to trust you're going in the right direction."
— Steven Aitchison

My perspective is important.

I will be heard.

I will hold the remote today!

I find strength in rooting to the earth,
for Mother Earth will hold space for me.

I will close my eyes tonight,
knowing I am satisfied today.

My feelings have names and must be recognized.

I have the power to create change in my life.

If I am not happy, I must do something.

"When one door of happiness closes, another opens; but often we look so long at the closed door that we do not see the one which has been opened for us."

— Helen Keller

I am calm and have peace of mind.

I am not responsible for anyone else's happiness.

I have the strength of my ancestors
in my bones and blood.

I dare to face what I don't want to.

I embrace my imperfections.

The world is a better place because I am in it.

I see joy and beauty in every day.

I am the master of my destiny.

Today, I will laugh and find humor.

I bless the past and look forward to the future.

I can have a soft heart
but still have firm boundaries.

I am human and all that it entails.

I am important.

I will make time for myself today and every day.

"Rise above the storm, and you will find the sunshine."
— Mario Fernández

I will say no to everyone and yes to me.

I will mourn all that I lost
without explanation to anyone.

I can hold two opposing feelings at once.

I breathe in peace and breathe out frustration.

I will grow at my own pace.

I am prepared for my dreams to come true.

I fill myself with optimism for a new day.

Today is a do-over.

"You are never too old to set another goal or to dream a new dream."

— C.S. Lewis

I breathe in trust and exhale doubt.

Words do not shape me. I shape myself.

Nothing can disturb my peace.

I will see synchronicities today
and know I am not alone.

I make time to feel grief
and sadness when I need to.

I am doing the work that's good for me.

I embrace tomorrow and all of its possibilities.

When I look ahead, I see sunrise, not sunset.

"Act as if what you do makes a difference. It does."
— William James

I trust myself.

Today, I will let go of the hurts of the past
and enjoy the freedom it brings.

The climb up the hill is as
exciting as the trip down.

I welcome prosperity.

I will not self-sabotage.

I am a spirit having a human experience.

Healing is within reach.

I am allowing my light to shine.

Negative thoughts only have
the power I give them.

I will not doubt myself or my integrity.

"I realized that I don't have to be perfect. All I have to do is show up and enjoy the messy, imperfect, and beautiful journey of my life."
— Kerry Washington

My greatest teacher is myself.

My heart is open to receive love.

I surrender my timeline to a higher power
and trust it will happen.

I release limiting beliefs about money and
accept the Universe's abundance in store for me.

"All our dreams can come true if we have the courage to pursue them."
— Walt Disney

I have pride in all my accomplishments.

Change is not a matter of doing but of accepting.

I am brave enough to do anything today.

There is something in the world that only
I can do, and that's why I exist.

Today, I will try something new.

I can be happy or sad. I am human.

I will not be told how to behave.

I set my expectations of myself.

"Success is a journey, not a destination."
— Ben Sweetland

I will do what makes me happy.

I will pack away all my worries and enjoy today.

I give stupidity back to those who dispense it.

If I want it, I will eat it.

I will not worry about tomorrow.
Only today exists.

I will make time for me and only me today.

I leave the past in the past.

I will enjoy the beauty that surrounds me.

Nothing can stop me from achieving my dreams.

Whatever I need to know will be revealed
at precisely the right time.

I release all my worries.

One hour at a time.
One step in front of each other.

I am capable of anything I desire.

I am grateful to be alive.

I release old habits that are limiting my potential.

I embrace doubt and discoveries.

I will learn something new today.

I challenge myself to face
negative people with grace.

I align with the good qualities
of the people around me.

I call on my Angel to help me when needed.

I understand that whatever my troubles are,
they will not last forever.

The future is in front of me, and I will look ahead.

"You've got to learn to leave the table when love's no longer being served."
— Nina Simone

I cannot control everything.

I have come far and have learned much.

I enjoy the constant change of life.

I will evolve.

I embrace what is and welcome what will be.

I give myself permission to grieve
for what I have lost.

I forget what does not serve my best interests.

I will work toward building a better community.

"Love yourself first, and everything else falls into place."
— Lucille Ball

If I don't understand,
I will still listen with an open heart.

I will let go of what doesn't serve me
to create space for new possibilities.

I will take daily action on what needs to be done.

Even if I can't see my loved ones,
I know I am not alone.

I have everything I need to succeed.

I will accept reality.

I am not afraid of growing old.

I will reinvent myself to match the changing times but not lose myself in the change.

"Believe you can, and you're halfway there."
— Theodore Roosevelt

My thoughts create reality
so that I will have positive thoughts.

I believe in my talents.

I will seek help if I need it.

My resilience makes me stronger.

I create my rules and live with the consequences.

I am worthy of my goals and dreams.

I encourage everyone around me with positive actions and thoughts.

I will not let anger paralyze me
and stop my growth.

Today, I will feed my spirit.

I will bring joy and happiness wherever I go.

I invite the wisdom of my elders to help me achieve my dreams.

I will let go of limiting beliefs.

I nourish myself with kind words.

I grow towards my interests like a sunflower
facing and reaching for the sun.

Asking for help is a sign of
self-awareness and self-respect.

If I don't like the direction I am going in,
I will change it.

I alone am in control of how I react to everything.

Everything is working in my favor.

I am not afraid of bumps in the road.
They make the journey more interesting.

I do not always have to be right.

Success can come in small wins.

"Change your thoughts, and you change your world."
— Norman Vincent Peale

I seek out the good news and share it.

I will be the pebble that creates ripples
of positive energy in the world.

I compare myself only to me and no one else.

I will not be held back by things that don’t matter.

Today, I will breathe deeply and enjoy my space.

I am me and am happy with who I am.

I stand by my beliefs and
am not ashamed of them.

I am my own best friend.

I am constantly generating new and fantastic ideas.

My wisdom keeps growing.

My life is not a race. It's a journey.

I am not afraid to stand up for myself.

"Above all, be the heroine of your life, not the victim."
— Nora Ephron

I am focused on the joys of my life.

Problems are opportunities to learn.

I will appreciate being still
and listening to my heart.

I will listen.

My needs and wants are important.

My purpose is to learn and grow.

I speak my truth and am proud of it.

I will be heard, even if I whisper.

I am a survivor.

"Our greatest glory is not in never falling, but in rising every time we fall."
— Confucius

I embrace discomfort because I will learn from it.

I will rest today.

There is always another choice.

I am free to create the world I desire.

I am unstoppable.

My mind is filled with
positive thoughts and feelings.

I hold space for others whether
they hold space for me or not.

I can do hard things.

Life doesn't happen to me. It happens for me.

My heart knows its way.

I will not be intimidated.

I am on a journey to becoming
the best version of myself.

I choose to live a healthy life.

I will protect myself physically,
emotionally, and spiritually.

I will resist anger. It serves no purpose.

I am brave enough to climb any mountain.

I invite abundance with joy into my life.

"If you cannot do great things, do small things in a great way."
— Napoleon Hill

I will not let criticism imprison me.

I am happy to live in an exciting time.

I embrace the peace
and quiet of restful sleep at night.

I will rise above pettiness.

I am content with my life
and patient with what is coming.

I will listen to my body.

I release generational trauma.

I will be truthful with others as well as myself.

I will not stay in the dark.

I will not let fear dictate my path.

I belong where I am.

I will do my best today.

I will not be pushed by my problems;
I will be inspired by my goals.

"Be a first-rate version of yourself,
instead of a second-rate version of somebody else."
— Judy Garland

I welcome new adventures.

I choose to surround myself with people who appreciate me.

I replace anger with compassion
and understanding.

I am on a journey where I am both
the passenger and creator.

I trust what the Universe has in store for me.

Age is a number and does not define my abilities.

"If you prioritize yourself, you are going to save yourself."

— Gabrielle Union

I embrace the changes in my body
as a roadmap for my life.

I've got this, and nothing will hold me back.

"I never dreamed about success. I worked for it."
— Estée Lauder

Resting is an integral part of working.

I choose happiness over being right.

I choose not to look back
but keep my gaze forward.

I will look for signs from the universe.

I will make healthy choices.

I am my own person and proud of who I am.

If I don't like something, I can change it.

I have a pure heart and pure intentions.

"Doubt kills more dreams than failure ever will."
— Suzy Kassem

I focus on the next step, not the entire path.

Healing takes time,
and I will have patience with myself.

Each day is a new beginning.

I will rise above anger and not let it pull me into its destructive embrace.

"Joy does not simply happen to us.
We have to choose joy and keep choosing it every day."
— Henri J.M. Nouwen

I am proud of myself.

I will learn something new today.

I release the need to be right.

I am a source of love for all those around me.

I accept responsibility for my mistakes
and forgive myself for them.

I am a member of the collective
and accept my place in it.

The Universe supports my success.

My calling is calling me.

"If you can dream it, you can do it."
— Walt Disney

I am surrounded by opportunities.

I will not let anyone minimize me.

I will expand my belief
from impossible to possible.

"Do something wonderful, people may imitate it."
— Albert Schweitzer

My life is filled with infinite possibilities.

I am rich in love and health.

I see beauty in everything from the tiniest cell
to the most prominent star.

I will guard myself against false compliments.

I grow stronger and more confident each day.

What I don't know or understand, I will learn.

Gossip benefits no one, and I will not help it grow.

I release disappointment and bitterness.

I will follow my dreams.

I am today years old.

I forgive myself and my past.

Growth can be challenging,
but I will stay the course.

Success is about the journey, not the destination.

I am committed to my personal growth.

I will not be offended by other's boundaries.

I will listen and hear what others need to tell me.

My sensitivity is personal to me.

My perspective is mine and doesn't have to be validated by anyone but me.

Even in my weirdness, I am wonderful.

I hold space for both your feelings and mine.

I have the right to believe in my opinion.

I am on the way to becoming my best self.

I believe in karma, and everything is working out how it should.

I will celebrate myself
and all I've accomplished today.

"What you get by achieving your goals is not as important as what you become by achieving your goals."
— Zig Ziglar

I don't have to explain my feelings to anybody.

I agree to disagree that we have different opinions that can be valid.

I will accept that I have done everything possible to fix something unfixable.

I am in the right place at the right time.

"If opportunity doesn't knock, build a door."
— Milton Berle

It will be what it should be,
which will work out for me.

My life is a gift, and I appreciate everything.

I will focus on what I am meant to do.

I will count my blessings today.

There is room for me at every table.

I am my highest priority.

I will focus on solutions, not the problems.

If it triggers me, I will avoid it.

My time is my own, and I will not squander it.

I will edit out the things that don't serve me.

"It always seems impossible until it's done."
— Nelson Mandela

I will discard painful reminders of my past.

I will pay attention to all my senses today.

I will watch the sunset just for me.

I will right the wrongs of my past.

I will find the positive in everyone.

I will not judge myself or others.

I can do anything I set my mind to.

I will not give anyone power over myself.

"For every minute you are angry, you lose sixty seconds of happiness."
— Ralph Waldo Emerson

I am invincible.

My disabilities are my superpower.

I will never give up.

There is more strength in speaking softly
than shouting to be heard.

I will step out of my comfort zone and grow.

Words have no power over me.

Only I can define who I am.

I am happy to be me
and not pretend to be anyone else.

I give myself permission to heal and be loved.

I allow myself to make mistakes.

"To improve is to change; to be perfect is to change often."
—Winston Churchill

I see abundance and success everywhere I look.

I bless the past and embrace the future.

I will face my fears with courage and confidence, knowing that I will find a way to overcome them.

I am leaping into my life with joy.

I am not threatened by anyone.

I am safe and protected by a greater good.

I am ready for anything that is coming.

I seek out positivity and surround myself with its white light.

"The only person you are destined to become is the person you decide to be."
— Ralph Waldo Emerson

I am constantly moving forward
toward my destiny.

I will redirect my thoughts
if they go in the wrong direction.

My riches are health, nature, and my loved ones.

I will wake up refreshed and ready for anything.

If I need an answer, the Universe will respond.

Music is there to fill me with joy.

I will balance my chakras
so I am running optimally.

I will connect to the Universe with my dreams.

I will allow nothing to disturb my peace.

I am capable of overcoming anything.

"Courage doesn't always roar. Sometimes, courage is the quiet voice at the end of the day saying, 'I will try again tomorrow'."
— Mary Anne Radmacher

I am filled with the white light of goodness,
which will protect me.

I have an aura of positivity around me.

I will not allow anyone to drain my energy.

I deserve to have my needs met.

I am motivated, focused, and capable.

I will balance the masculine
and feminine energies within me.

There is no limit to my goals.

I will heal myself and not rely
on the comfort of others.

I have confidence in everything I do.

The success I seek is waiting for me.

I will allow myself to be comforted.

I am a shining light and a beacon for others.

I celebrate all people and their differences.

I am complete by myself.

I am on a journey for me.

"The moment you doubt whether you can fly, you cease forever to be able to do it."

— J.M. Barrie

I am listening and open to learning from others.

Author's Note

I hope this book of inspirational quotes and affirmations helps you through the dips and valleys of life. They are a collection of my interpretations of the wisdom of the ages. Collected from a diverse group spanning generations, it has played a huge role and influenced me throughout the decades.

Each reflects different periods of my life, struggles in school with learning disabilities, weight issues, and learning to set boundaries, even with those I loved. They have bolstered me up when I found no one was listening. My fight with cancer, the setbacks of illness that devastated my family, and losses of all kinds left me baffled and unsure how to handle myself.

I think of them as permission slips. Personal messages that remind us to take care of ourselves, not to forget what matters, and, most importantly, to accept the changes in a way that helps us grow and enjoy life to the fullest.

They have held me steady through stormy seas. Sensible ideas and reminders that anchored me when I was adrift in a sea of uncertainty.

I have sprinkled them like fairy dust for my friends and family when they felt defeated by life's challenges. They have always inspired me to dust myself off and try again. I have no regrets.

I have discovered that the hardest of times tempers us like steel and lets us know how strong we truly are.

May your hopes and dreams take flight, and let no one stand in your way.

Shine on.

Phyllis Okon
Long Island, 2023

ABOUT THE AUTHOR

Phyllis Okon is a gifted medium and psychic.

She has traveled many roads until finally finding this path. A teacher, CEO, best-selling and award-winning author, wife, mother, and grandmother have all contributed to establishing her as a compassionate and understanding medium.

Her ability to connect and give evidential information proves she has been guided by all the best teachers in the field.

She has studied with many well-known leaders in mediumship, including Kim Russo, Richard Knight, and Joseph Shiel.

From an early age, Phyllis acknowledged that she knew things but could never explain how she did.

Busy raising her family, and building her business alongside her husband, she finally entered the publishing world in her mid-fifties. As authors Carole P. Roman and Brit Lunden, she successfully published over eighty books in different genres. Many of them went on to win numerous awards. Her Big Book of Silly Jokes outsold every book on Amazon and held the number one spot for over two months.

It wasn't until her lifelong partner, her husband, passed that she began taking courses in mediumship to communicate with him.

She learned that her relationship with her soulmate didn't end, and her husband jumped in to serve as a guide, helping her connect others with their loved ones. "He was my help-meet in life and is the same from the other side."

Genuine, loving, and eager to provide the same solace she receives when she gets messages, a session with Phyllis gives a lifetime of comfort.

"Affirmations are the foundation of my life and have shaped the highs by elevating me from the lows."

Printed in the USA
CPSIA information can be obtained
at www.ICGtesting.com
JSHW051241081223
53082JS00007B/154

9 781950 080137